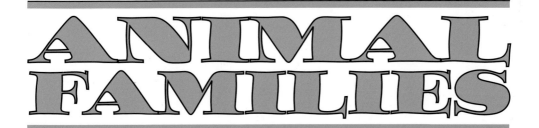

ANIMAL FAMILIES

Daisy Allyn

REAL LIFE readers™

Rosen Classroom™

New York

This is a dog family.

The mother is big.

The puppy is small.

This is a cat family.

The mother is big.

The kitten is small.

Here is a chicken.

Here is a chick.

Which is the mother?

Which is the baby?

Here is a bear.

Here is a cub.

Which is the mother?

Which is the baby?

Look at the cow.

Look at the calf.

Which is the mother?

Which is the baby?

ANIMAL FAMILES

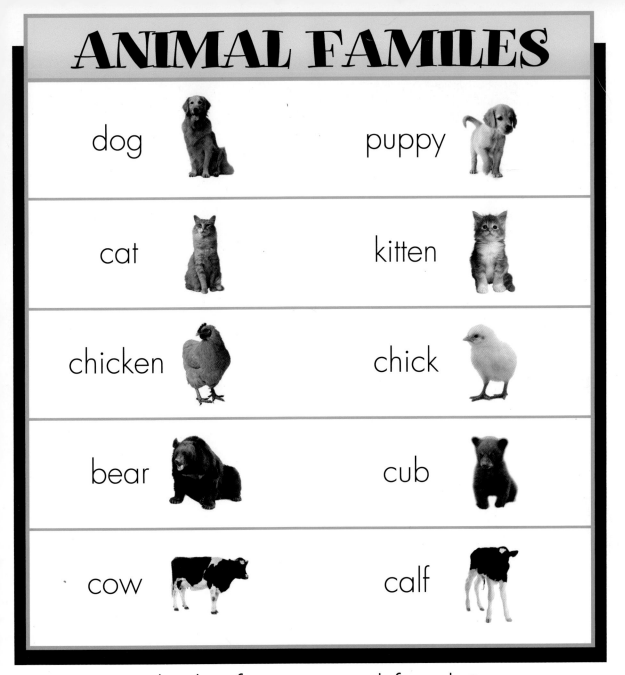

dog   puppy

cat   kitten

chicken   chick

bear   cub

cow   calf

Can you think of an animal family?

WORDS TO KNOW

bear

calf

cat

chick

chicken

cow

cub

dog

kitten

puppy